HOW TO LIVE TO
100

SECRETS FROM THE WORLD'S HAPPIEST CENTENARIANS

Dr. Elizabeth Lopez

Leaders
Press

ISBN (paperback) 978-1-943386-55-0
ISBN (hardcover) 978-1-943386-56-7
ISBN (ebook) 978-1-943386-54-3

Library of Congress Control Number: 2019909515

Interior Artwork: Couple's Dance by Lillianne Ruiz Truque.
Acrylic on Canvas. 80 x 65 cm. 2018.
Design and layout: Priscila Coto
Photography: Cristina E. Díaz and Jorge Vindas

To the great young loves
in my life:

Javi,

Andy,

Emily,

Marisia,

Manrique,

Fernando,

Amanda,

Tomas,

Ashby

and Tai

— may they all live to be

100

Contents

Elizabeth Lopez was on my original National Geographic team that discovered the blue zone in Nicoya, Costa Rica. She worked side by side with me as we teased out the factors that produced arguably the world's longest-living people. A Costa Rican herself and trained as a psychologist, she was uniquely qualified to assess Nicoya's longevity All-Stars and identify the social determinants of their extraordinary health. Here she's written a beautiful book that offer lessons for anyone wanting to live a longer, healthier life.

Dan Buettner,
National Geographic Fellow, *New York Times* Bestseller
and Founder of Blue Zones

Latest estimates are that someone born today has a 50/50 chance of living to 100. For the rest of us, Dr. Lopez has put together an excellent guide, based on research and in-depth interviews, for leading lives that might, just might, enable us to all to live to 100. The recipes, both figuratively and literally are all contained in this marvelous book.

Doug Smith,
author of *Happiness: The Art of Living with Peace, Confidence and Joy*

In this book, Elizabeth adds convincing new insight into the reasons why Nicoya's Costa Rican centenarians achieve such remarkable longevity when, like millions of people in many countries throughout the world, they were born and lived more than their first 60 years in a poor and isolated region with water that wasn't always safe, food that was not always adequate, limited protection from insects and the elements, and high infant mortality. Elizabeth shows they achieved this to a significant extent because of their relatively stress-free culture and the strong social support it provided, as well as their optimistic and happy personalities. Elizabeth's previous personal experience and professional background provide a solid foundation for writing this contribution to understanding healthy aging.

Dr. Rogelio Pardo,
former Minister of Public Health, Costa Rica

Dr. Elizabeth Lopez has in an impressive way made use of face-to-face conversations with Costa Rica's centenarians to add amazing new insights into how culture and personality contribute significantly to the remarkable longevity of these people. In addition, the book effectively portrays the richness of Costa Rican culture and analyzes how it impacts everyday life. She has successfully improved the methodology of conducting face-to-face interviews.

Her direct, richly anecdotal and empathetic interaction with a target population sample provides the reader with a firsthand view into how they can use their culture and personality to improve longevity. It gives real-life awareness as to how readers can achieve increased longevity by reducing stress in their lives and by living a simpler life.

The book provides insight and hope by learning from those living more than 100 years as to how we could live longer healthier and happier lives; a lesson most of us need to understand better. The book clearly shows that it is up to us to make the choices that will allow us to have longer, healthier and happier lives.

Could Dr. Lopez's insights change enough peoples' behavior to contribute to increasing longevity statistically? Let's pay close attention!

Dr. Enrique Madrigal,
M.D. CIMA Psychiatrist

Foreword

This book, *How to Live to 100*, is opportune as its message is essential reading for these times as millions of people have or soon will reach the 'older adult' stage. The research it contains provides hope and a feeling of looking forward to old age. It offers concrete examples of how real happiness and healthy lifestyles are achieved at these late life stages.

The first section of the book conveys a profound understanding of what Dr. Lopez calls "the golden years" as she provides a number of concrete portraits of successful aging as a platform for her subsequent innovative insights and theory as to how centenarians, through their culture and personalities, enhance personal longevity. She achieves this objective so effectively that reading the book will provide wisdom, hope and guidance for those of us who are aging.

In the second section, Elizabeth uses her extensive experience as a social scientist, psychologist and member of the Blue Zones™ scientific team, as well as her personal involvement in the centenarian interviews in the field, to provide convincing concrete examples in support of her conclusions that culture and personality have a significant impact on longevity.

Every centenarian interviewed demonstrates the irreplaceable value of good interpersonal relationships that go far beyond close family relationships to include close relationships with neighbors and the whole community. It leads readers to ask themselves have we moved the invaluable contributions that close healthy relationships with those near to us, fundamental human emotions and appreciation of nature, all of which enrich our lives with enjoyment, happiness and fulfillment, too far to the back burner. The book provides valuable advice for how to enhance personal longevity by moving these invaluable elements of our lives to the front burner.

Dr. Rose Marie Karpinsky,
Former President of the Congress of Costa Rica

Preface

Ten years ago, on a breezy, sunny afternoon, I was reading a local newspaper and learned that a group of international scientists was coming to Costa Rica on an expedition to study an unusually large group of centenarians in Costa Rica's Nicoya Peninsula. They wanted to verify whether this area was a true 'blue zone' and if so, why. The team had earlier coined the name 'blue zone' for those few areas in the world where the percentage of verifiable centenarians is higher than anywhere else.

Was it a true blue zone? Yes! A section of Costa Rica's Nicoya Peninsula has the second highest number of centenarians as a percentage of the population of any place in the world. The expedition's main objective was to discover why so many people there lived so long.

The Blue Zones™[1] team has now identified five such areas in the world namely Sardinia, Italy (with the highest proportion of centenarians in the world); Nicoya Peninsula, Costa Rica; Okinawa, Japan; Loma Linda, California; and Ikaria, Greece. It would almost seem as if the centenarians in these

---

1   Blue Zones is a registered trademark of Blue Zones LLC

blue zones have made up their minds not to die; they continue having birthdays for many years even after reaching the 100-year landmark.

After reading the article, I decided to call Dr. Luis Rosero Bixby, its author and the Director of the Central American Population Center at the University of Costa Rica, to find out how I could join the Blue Zones™ expedition mentioned in the article. He put me in touch with Dan Buettner, owner and CEO of Blue Zones LLC, Inc., who would be leading it.[2] Dan called me, interviewed me by phone, and agreed to my becoming a member of the team. Four days later, filled with excitement and anticipation, I was meeting the research team in front of the Catholic church in the Costa Rican city of Nicoya, located on the peninsula of the same name in the province of Guanacaste.

I am a Costa Rican psychologist with more than 40 years of professional experience, working not on the dysfunctionalities that we as human beings may have but on our strengths and how we can use them to improve our lives. I am a well-being psychologist.

I grew up in Costa Rica but lived in the United States for a total of 30 years, first as an adolescent, then as a young adult, and yet again working there until I retired and returned to Costa Rica. My work experience includes positions such as

---

2   This Costa Rica Blue Zone expedition was financed by National Geographic and CNN. It took place in February 2007.

counseling psychologist, university professor, international presenter and consultant and — the most interesting of all my jobs — working for the World Bank in Washington, D.C. for 15 years as a Senior Human Resources Counselor. My American husband and I currently have homes in Costa Rica and Reston, Virginia.

Having always been deeply interested in culture, I wrote my Ed.D. dissertation on a "Comparative Study of Four Cultural Groups in Psychosocial Development and Locus of Control." My interest in longevity is based on my life-long passion for knowledge in the areas of human development, the relationship between personality and culture, cross-cultural comparisons, and how to improve human lives. I have dedicated my professional life to sharing this knowledge with other people interested in living longer, healthier, happier and more fulfilling lives. This book was written with the objective of helping people live longer, more happily and in a more youthful way.

My interest in Guanacaste and the Nicoya Peninsula centenarians isn't just a quest for knowledge and wisdom; it is also because my dear mother was born in Guanacaste and spent her childhood there. The first time I remember visiting Guanacaste was when I was 4 years old. Since then, I have often visited the Nicoya Peninsula, Guanacaste and the many beautiful towns and beaches in this part of Costa Rica.

That morning on an expedition ten years ago, I began what has proved to be one of the richest and most interesting adventures in my whole professional life. I was given the opportunity to work as the psychologist on the Blue Zones™ research team. The team, well-suited for studying why Nicoya's centenarians lived so long, was composed of Dan Buettner, a writer and researcher, Michelle Poulain, a demographer, and Gianni Pes, a gerontologist, along with a science writer, photographers, nutritionists, research assistants, reporters and, yes, a very excited Costa Rican psychologist.

The team's findings were presented in the New York Times bestselling book *The Blue Zones: Lessons for Living Longer from the People Who've Lived the Longest*. Dan Buettner and his team have built on that foundation with several additional books, an extremely useful website complete with regular emails outlining health-related advice, and the development of a blue zones lifestyle concept that is in the process of being adopted by a growing number of communities both in the U.S. and abroad.

His book presents many extremely useful insights on diet, exercise and other factors common to all the blue zones (including Nicoya) that contributed to longevity. It also includes my observations on the psychological factors that enhanced longevity for Nicoya's centenarians. Among these were having a purpose in life and feeling needed, being deeply religious, and having a strong human support network composed of both family and friends.

In February 2017, I resumed the quest to gain a better understanding of the psychological and cultural factors contributing to the mystery of why Nicoya's centenarians lived longer than people almost everywhere else. I returned to Nicoya with a research assistant, Jorge Vindas, to continue my research, interviewing more centenarians and knowledgeable area residents on a topic that is of great interest to me as a psychologist — the relationship between personality characteristics, culture and longevity and whether or not this relationship is causal.

This book is based on the information provided directly by the centenarians during face-to-face interviews in their homes and their everyday environments. We sat on wooden stools and benches under mango trees, on their porches or in their living rooms talking with them and their families, usually while listening to a concert of tropical birdsongs and looking at the big trees surrounding their homes. The findings in this book are also based on my interactions with groups, families, street and market vendors, restaurant owners, seniors attending their daily meetings at the community senior center, and knowledgeable professionals living in the area. We drove to a number of different rural villages to visit the centenarians in their homes and the everyday environment in which they have lived for decades.

Most of the information and insights in this book were collected on my trip to the blue zone with the invaluable assistance of Jorge Vindas, a knowledgeable field research assistant with Blue Zones LLC Inc, who is very well known in the area by the centenarians, their families and whole communities as he visits them regularly.

This book attempts to convey a feeling for the Costa Rica's blue zone's centenarians' personalities, amazing culture, lifestyles, beliefs, faith and religious practices that have been around for centuries. All these factors contribute to explaining how the lead actors in this book, the centenarians, lived to be 100 or more and what we can learn from how they have done it. It also attempts to share some of the magic and charm encompassed in our conversations with the centenarians and their families in their homes, the Nicoyan communities and the beautiful natural environment.

The centenarians' personalities, beliefs, lifestyle and culture seem to have impacted their physical, social, psychological and spiritual wellbeing in ways that have allowed them to live relatively stress-free lives filled with positivity, physical stamina, enjoyment of life, close family ties, a sense of feeling needed and valued, faith and overall happiness. These amazing people have been thinking, doing and behaving over the many years in ways that give them little basis for worrying about their ages or the fact that they will eventually die.

The book covers aspects of Costa Rican culture, especially Guanacastecan culture,[3] which contribute to the centenarians' long and relatively stress-free lives, including family relationships, attitudes toward the elderly, religion, spirituality,

---

3   Guanacastecans, in addition to sharing many cultural characteristics common to all Costa Ricans, have a distinct subculture as they were part of Nicaragua for many years until becoming a remote Costa Rica province, until recently hard to get to from the rest of the country.

humor, stress management, happiness, societal practices, pride in regional identity, and the unique 'Pura Vida' attitude toward life for which Costa Rica is famous. Costa Rican culture is a vital part of the package contributing to the remarkable longevity of these people.

Finally, this book offers the reader ideas for making possible life changes in practices and behaviors that can lead to longer, healthier, more fulfilling lives. Readers will also have easy access in the annex to recipes for some of the key dishes and foods that these centenarians have been eating for many years.

The book provides examples of good, well-lived, long lives which, if we learn from them, can help us make simple future choices in everyday life that can lead to longer, healthier and happier years ahead.

The Magic of Nicoya

This book begins where the blue zone's centenarians were born and have lived all their lives, the Nicoya Peninsula. It briefly describes the magic of the Nicoya Peninsula's environment by way of its geography, history, climate, culture and lifestyle before introducing the reader to some of its most interesting centenarians.

The Nicoya Peninsula, part of the province of Guanacaste, is located in the northwestern part of the country. Guanacaste is a vast area (about 3,900 square miles with a population of 354,000) that was originally part of Nicaragua, not Costa Rica.[4] Following negotiations with the political authorities in both countries, however, the residents of Guanacaste voted to become part of Costa Rica in 1824.

Guanacaste has historically been the home of the Chorotega people. At the time of the Spanish conquest, the Chorotegans were the largest and most technologically advanced ethnic group in Costa Rica.[5] They were living in this area

---

4   The Nicoya Peninsula, where the centenarians live, has an area of 415 square miles and a projected 2018 population of 185,845 people.

5   According to the Encyclopedia Britannica.

long before being colonized but were to a significant extent decimated by the Spaniards. Some were sent by the Spaniards as slaves to work in other parts of Latin America. The Chorotegans were artistic and culturally different from other ethnic groups inhabiting Costa Rica at that time. Many of Nicoya's centenarians have at least some or in some cases, even a predominant, Chorotegan ancestry.

All of Guanacaste, even more so the Nicoya Peninsula, was isolated for many years from the rest of Costa Rica as infrastructure and communications systems made connecting with the capital or other big cities very difficult. Visitors to the area were only able to get to Guanacaste by first taking a train, then crossing the Gulf of Nicoya by boat and finally riding horseback to their final destination. This isolation and remoteness allowed the inhabitants of the peninsula to keep their own unique cultural traditions and sense of identity intact to a significant extent.

When I was growing up, I remember my mother, a Guanacastecan, telling me stories about when she was attending high school in San José (Costa Rica's capital and biggest city) but spending summer vacations in Liberia, Guanacaste. In order to get from San José to her grandma's house in Liberia (the capital and largest city of Guanacaste), she had to take a train for several hours, then a boat for several more, until she got to Bebedero, a port in Guanacaste, and then had to continue on a horse or an ox cart for many more hours.

A Guanacastecan has been described in a book on Guanacaste and its people[6] as "by nature, a good host of cheerful character, talkative person and of great imagination. The Guanacastecans like to dance, like music and the romantic serenades. Has special attraction for the guitar, the marimba and lives with deep intensity the celebrations of his towns."

It is easy to fall in love with the rivers, mountains, beautiful beaches, sunsets, flora and fauna of Guanacaste. Some of its birds and local fruits are found nowhere else in Costa Rica. The exuberant environment together with a common regional history give Guanacastecans a strong sense of identity and pride in being from the area.

For Nicoya's centenarians, the environmental setting and strong sense of regional identity have interacted with their culture, diet, lifestyles and personalities to provide a foundation for their remarkable longevity. It has also given them a deep love for the beautiful nature around them.

6   *Guanacaste, Life and Culture* by Carlos Arauz Ramos.

2 Culture and Personality

Culture

Culture is the pattern of thinking, feeling and acting of a group of people or an individual. It is defined by some as "the software of the mind."[7] It is a fundamental force that plays an important role in fostering the Nicoya centenarians' lifestyle and molding their personalities. And the evidence suggests that the culture of Costa Rica, even more so its Guanacastecan subculture, plays a significant role in longevity.

Costa Rica is a collectivistic culture and society that avoids conflict, has a strong sense of community, and within which religion and community play fundamentally important roles.

Nicoya's centenarians have lived all their lives in a highly collectivistic society, which means they see the well-being of the whole group as more important to its members than the well-being of an individual. Even their self-identity is collectivistic. They have a strong tendency to see themselves

---

7   As mentioned in *Cultures and Organizations: Software of the Mind* by Geert Hofstede, 1991.

more as who they are related to and what groups they are part of than who they are as individuals or what work they do or did. Therefore, members of their social groups tend to be generous with each other, help others achieve goals, care deeply about families and friendships, and avoid conflict.

Saúl Guzmán's family

As in other collectivistic cultures, the Nicoya centenarians' family relationships are very strong, resulting in their receiving care and attention from other family members almost around the clock. They receive messages from other family members that they are loved and respected from other family members on a regular basis, thus providing a sense of security and importance. This is further enriched with virtually daily social interaction with friends as well as family members.

The attitude toward conflict avoidance which permeates most relationships leads to a sense of peacefulness and minimizes one important source of stress. Indeed, this attitude toward conflict avoidance is even reflected at the national level as Costa Rica is widely known to be peace-loving; President Óscar Arias, reflecting national values in his policies, won a Nobel Peace Prize.

It is a present-oriented society in which there is little time pressure. A tendency toward being fatalistic combines with a strong belief that the future will be good. This orientation and a widespread confidence that God will protect them are a potent stress-reduction mechanism. Interpersonal relationships are based on strong family and social-network support systems known for warmth, empathy and a willingness to provide help when needed. The centenarians, like most of the elderly in Nicoya, have their self-esteem and sense of self-importance bolstered almost daily as they are widely treated with love and respect no matter how old they are and how physically frail they may have become. Moreover, their reciprocal role in providing advice and, when they can, help to the younger family members and those around them provides a sense of purpose and service that also contributes to living longer.

As for perception of time, present-oriented societies share a general attitude that there is little need to worry about how much time something is taking, that there is no need to hurry, and that the future does not need to be planned as rigorously as in more future-oriented societies. Consequently, the pace of life tends to be relaxed. This relaxation is even further accentuated by the often hot weather which can drain energy and slow physical movement, especially in the middle of the day. Nicoya is a present-oriented society with relatively little time pressure and a decidedly relaxed way of dealing with day-to-day life.

José Bonifacio Villegas

The role of the Catholic Church throughout Costa Rica cannot be underestimated as it is pervasive and most citizens have historically been Catholics. In Nicoya, Catholic churches have been built in virtually every town, even very small ones. In small towns, they are often located in front of the soccer field and are part of the town center where most businesses and much of the social activity takes place.

Foto: © Cristina E. Díaz

Nicoya Colonial Church

Therefore, the centenarians have lived their whole lives in Catholic-centered communities and have, almost without exception, a strong faith in God, and they value spirituality.

This, together with a widespread belief that God will protect them, leads to a firm belief that the future will be good.

Culture, of course, has a huge impact on the centenarians' lifestyle. And their lifestyle, so convincingly presented in Buettner's book on the Blue Zones, is a healthy one in many respects, including diet and exercise as well as work, recreation, sleep habits and time spent outdoors.

These collectivistic, present-oriented cultural aspects and religion, together with associated lifestyle and personality elements, can be encapsulated in a unique philosophy of life for which Costa Rica is famous. One hears the name for this philosophy, 'Pura Vida',[8] directly translated into English as 'Pure Life,' repeated almost daily by citizens of all ages and economic levels everywhere in Costa Rica. Pura Vida is both a philosophy and a way of life that symbolizes the idea of enjoying life and being happy and relatively carefree. It effectively summarizes a predominant Costa Rican attitude, shared by Nicoya's centenarians, toward lifestyle, happiness, well-being, conformity and satisfaction. It tends to result in a blissful, peaceful, uncluttered and relatively stress-free life

8   According to Wikipedia, Pura Vida is a characteristic Costa Rican phrase, literally meaning 'pure life' with connotations that suggest translations such as 'full of life,' 'this is living,' 'going great' and 'real living'. The phrase can be used both as a greeting or a farewell, as an answer expressing that things are going well, and as a way of giving thanks or showing appreciation. In modern-day usage, the saying goes beyond its simple translation: it's a way of life. It is a perspective on life that evokes a spirit that is carefree, laid-back and optimistic.

with a deep appreciation for nature, family, friends and day-to-day human interaction.

Nicoya's relative geographic isolation has historically intensified the impact of culture on the centenarians as it has limited outside influences that would have, and in the future in all likelihood will, dilute the culture and its impact. [9]

Personality

Personality is the combination of three factors that a person exhibits — thoughts, emotions and behaviors. Together, they determine who we are, what we think, how we feel and how we behave. These factors are heavily influenced by the culture within which people live, as it is a predominant force in shaping the personality of both the group and the individuals within it.

9   It is interesting to note that the other blue zones in Sardinia, Icaria (Greece) and Okinawa are all in places that were relatively isolated geographically until recently. While the other blue zone, Loma Linda California, is not geographically isolated, the strong presence of Seventh-day Adventists and their role are likely to have intensified the impact of culture on its centenarians.

Personality Traits/Characteristics Exhibited

Do personality characteristics predict longevity? Research in a documented Japanese study, *The Tokyo Centenarian Study*[10] concluded that the answer is "Yes"; there is a longevity personality. People who are optimistic and easy-going live longer. The study focused on five traits believed to be personality-related predictors of longevity — low neuroticism (which includes anxiety, depression and vulnerability), high extroversion (which includes activity, excitement-seeking and positive emotions), openness, agreeableness and conscientiousness. These findings suggest that personality has the fourth most important role in increasing longevity after genetic, physical and biological factors.

Most of Nicoya's interviewed centenarians exhibit several personality traits and characteristics that reduce stress and demonstrate extroversion. These include optimistic thinking, external attribution style[11], self-efficacy, excitement seeking, positive emotion, agreeableness and openness. These personality patterns, in all likelihood often inextricably linked with culture, were found to be remarkably consistent among these centenarians.

---

10   Written by Y. Masui, Y. Gondo, H. Ingaki and N. Hirose and dated June 6, 2006.

11   External attribution style is defined as how we meet our need to explain what happens in the world around us with a tendency to attribute cause to events, giving reasons for why things occur.

These centenarians commonly display three other personality characteristics/traits, competence, self-discipline and deliberation, which are indicators of a trait called conscientiousness. These traits were consistently revealed in many of the interviews by repeated references to two characteristics — pride in ability to take care of oneself and a disciplined approach to following directions for taking medications and doing what was needed to maintain the best health possible.

Jose Bonifacio Villegas in his back yard

Virtually all the interviewed centenarians showed personality characteristics that are closely linked to Costa Rica's Pura Vida collectivistic culture, including happiness, humor, respect for elders, generosity, and being a dependable source of help for others. These centenarians also all had a strong sense of regional and personal identity.

In a wonderful book entitled *Happiness*,[12] Douglas Smith says that "happiness is an attitude, a way of looking at the world, a perspective. It is not circumstances of pleasure, it is not a mood, it is not fleeting or ephemeral, it is not frivolous or unworthy. Rather, it is at the core of our existence. People who are happy can return to the core again and again even in times of turmoil and adversity."

This could just as easily be said about Costa Rica's Pura Vida culture. I found all the centenarians I talked with to be happy, and being happy is certainly one secret to their longevity. In a chapter on Costa Rica in Dan Buettner's book on happiness[13], he refers to Costa Rica as one of the world's happiest countries because "Costa Ricans excel at getting the most joy out of their days." He goes on to say that for Costa Ricans a powerful blend of family bonds, universal health care, faith, peace, equality and generosity culminate in an especially rich recipe for enjoying life day by day — the strand of happiness he calls "pleasure". All the Nicoyan centenarians I interviewed are generous, happy personalities that fit Dan's description of Costa Ricans of all ages extraordinarily well.

12 *Happiness* by Douglas Smith. Published by White Pine Mountain, 2014.

13 *The Blue Zones of Happiness* by Dan Buettner. Published by National Geographic Partners, LLC, 2017

3 How They Live

The 2007 Blue Zones™ Costa Rica expedition concluded that centenarian lifestyles, with their focus on diet and exercise, have a major impact on longevity. Other aspects of lifestyle,[14] including work, sleep, relaxation and recreation, also have an impact. My subsequent interviews with centenarians led me to parallel conclusions.

Diet

The centenarians' diet throughout their lives can be described as simple, repetitive, nutritious and reasonably well-balanced. All of them reported that their main staple has been rice and beans, commonly known as gallo pinto, sometimes eaten for every meal, every day, or served by separating the rice from the beans. Other foods commonly eaten include maize (corn), fresh vegetables that are produced in the area, including ayote (traditional squash) as well as other types

---

14 According to the Webster dictionary, lifestyle is defined as a particular way of living, the way a person lives, or how a group of people live.

of squash, chayote (a vegetable pear), potatoes, carrots, fruit, whole milk, eggs, meat, poultry and some fish.

Farmers Market

Work

All the centenarians had worked very hard, mostly outdoors, since early on in their lives. The majority, both men and women, worked in the fields, often from very early morning to mid or late afternoon without the aid of tractors or sophisticated machinery. They were often at work in the fields at 6 a.m. until the ages of 80 or even 90 years old.

José Bonifacio Villegas

Men would always work in the field or herd cattle. Women would often work in the fields helping their partners or husbands. They also cooked for the family and other people who were working on their farms, while simultaneously raising children.

Exercise

Exercise came with the territory as the hard work in the fields and walking out of necessity to and from work, school and/or the market or pulpería[15] constituted daily exercise. Some centenarians had to leave their homes at four in the morning to get to work by 6 after having walked several miles and would, at the end of the day, walk that same distance back. Much of their working and some of their walking was done under the hot Guanacaste sun as their work was virtually always outside. Some of them rode horses that would take them to their work out in the fields. They never needed an exercise program or visits to a gym as substantial exercise was inherent in how they made a living and brought food to their homes.

15   Pulperías are small convenience stores.

Sleep

Sleep patterns are largely determined by the sun. Consequently, most of the centenarians would now be viewed as 'larks' as for their whole lives they have usually gone to bed early, at 8 or 9 p.m., and risen very early in the morning. Of course, exceptions were and are made for the not infrequent parties filled with music and dancing, sometimes almost to dawn.

Recreation and Relaxation

In Nicoya, relaxation and recreation have been combined in one favorite activity, an often-recurring mix that includes social dancing, guitar playing and socializing in groups with the community, neighborhood families and friends or just the family. It has been a tradition here that families, often with friends, start gathering together around 4 o'clock in the afternoon and they usually begin the socializing with coffee, fresh fruit drinks and pastries made mainly from cornmeal to accompany the coffee. In the centenarians' homes, children (often in their eighties), grandchildren, great-grandchildren and friends begin to gather around the centenarians, typically several afternoons each week to spend time with them, listen to their stories, and learn from them as well as sharing family stories of what happened during the day either at work, in their homes or at their schools. While there may be some talk about politics, it is never as serious as the more serious discussions about soccer and their favorite teams.

According to one of Costa Rica's leading authorities on geriatrics, the most popular sport for both men and women in Costa Rica is dancing whenever the opportunity may present itself, whether at parties, in saloons or just for the fun of it. It seems this activity involves even more people than soccer. It is not uncommon in Costa Rica to find dancing saloons even in small towns and remote places; Nicoya is no exception. Dancing is a relaxing, fun, socially-engaging, stress-reducing exercise in which even centenarians can participate.

Saúl Guzmán

Foto: © Cristina E. Díaz

4 Centenarian Portraits, Life Histories and Personalities

I can think of no better way to describe the Nicoya centenarians' life histories, culture and personalities than by using their own words, derived from my conversations with them and supplemented by observations from a few knowledgeable individuals who know them well. They are presented here in the form of short individual self-portraits.

Therefore, as preparation for this book, Jorge Vindas and I conversed with seven centenarians, usually in their home or place of business, in several communities. We interviewed centenarians and their families, attended a birthday party, interviewed a community leader where centenarians lived, and in my case, received two marriage proposals from centenarians who obviously felt younger than their years. The following vignettes portray the seven centenarians who were particularly interesting or whose answers were particularly instructive input in my search for personality and culture-related secrets of longevity in the blue zone of Costa Rica. In addition, one man who was only 95 is featured, partly because his mother died last year aged 110, who were particularly interesting or whose answers were particularly instructive input in my search, for personality and culture-related secrets of longevity in the blue zone of Costa Rica.

Each vignette begins with a direct quotation or two that highlight personalities or lifestyles that are particularly interesting or instructive and each ends with an observation as to what I saw as the most striking culture and/or personality aspects of each centenarian.

Foto: © Cristina E. Díaz

José Bonifacio Villegas Fonseca

100 years old. Quebrada Honda, Nicoya

"When I get pain, I get on a horse, ride for a while and all the pain goes away."

"I have given all my possessions to my children, so I do not have to worry about those things."

The landscape on the Nicoya Peninsula and on our drive to José's house is breathtaking, especially in the morning when the sun seems to bring out every color and shade of green on the trees and the bright tropical colors of the wild flowers and of all the nature on which it is shining. Many beautiful birds are easily spotted, and one can hear their concert of harmonizing and discordant calls in a seemingly-simultaneous performance. Early morning is a time of day when the mountains and plains vibrate with energy and invite us all to enjoy life.

As we were driving on a narrow, dirt road, we spotted, far in the distance, a man coming toward us riding on a horse and Jorge Vindas exclaimed, "This guy coming on the horse is José Bonifacio, the centenarian that we will be interviewing early this afternoon." As the gentleman approached the car, it was obvious that he was tall and slender, with brown-colored skin, good posture and in apparent total control of all his muscles as well as of the tall, strong horse that he was riding. We stopped our car and Bonifacio pulled to a stop next to our window. Without getting down from the horse, he greeted us with a warm, friendly smile and happily shared with us that he was heading back to his home having visited some of his friends. He had left his house at 9 a.m. and was obviously still alert and energetic two hours later. We agreed with Bonifacio that we would be back at his home at 2 p.m. as planned.

That afternoon, we found the house that was surrounded by many big trees. There was also a turkey running around and a green parrot. There were parakeets coming to the back porch to feed before returning to the trees. Rather than going to his front door, we went around the back to the porch and found Bonifacio and some of his children, friends and grandchildren seated there waiting for us.

They were sitting on informal chairs closely facing each other on the porch, which, while about 12 feet long, was only 6 feet wide. While the family looked relaxed, they were obviously curious to find out what our real motives for being there were. They kindly offered us chairs and we explained that we were interested in talking with Bonifacio about his life. We told him that we were pleased that there was also a big group of his family and friends to interact with. As in all the interviews, we emphasized that it was an informal conversation, not a formal interview, and the purpose was to learn from the centenarians in Nicoya about their lifestyle, their philosophy of life, and their life in general from childhood to the present. I mentioned that I was gathering information to write a book about the centenarians' lifestyles so that other people in foreign countries could learn some of the secrets as to how they lived so long.

Bonifacio and his group, as with all the other centenarians I interviewed, felt complimented and pleased that we thought they were important enough to talk to and were very forthcoming, indeed eager, to respond as fully as they could in answer to our questions.

Bonifacio sat comfortably in a chair at the end of one of the two rows arranged on the porch. He had a clean and well-pressed colored shirt and khaki pants. Although he is 100 years old, when he walks, his gait is strong, his lean muscles can be easily seen, and his vision seems fine. He is friendly and talkative, and smiles and grins often.

Like many centenarians, Bonifacio comes from a large family, as he is one of 11 children. He grew up with his father and stepmothers. He commented that stepmothers are always ugly as he can attest to having had several of them. His mother died when he was six and his father had several different relationships. Several of his older siblings left the house at relatively young ages (between 15 and 20) but he stayed at home until the age of 28 when his father died because he loved his father dearly. Bonifacio takes great pride in that fact. After mourning his father's death, he felt very lonely and married two years later at the age of 30. He then had eight children.

Unlike his friends, he rode a horse to school, which he attended up to third grade. He would leave his home at 7 a.m. and be back by noontime. He commented that the teachers were very strict and that "they managed him with a tight leash." He was subject to tough discipline both at home and at school and had a rough upbringing. He had to ask permission to do almost anything until he was 15, after which he became a little bit more independent.

Bonifacio has always loved being in groups and being surrounded by people. His family and friends come every afternoon to enjoy themselves and have coffee or drinks (which sometimes include alcohol) on his back porch. There's always a toast and lots of fun. He has always liked to dance,

José Bonifacio Villegas

still dances but has stopped drinking alcohol, and is a happy camper. He thanks God that he has always been very friendly and has always had lots of friends.

There are smaller houses surrounding Bonifacio's home where his children live, and family members move back and forth between those houses and his throughout the day. The parcels of land where Bonifacio's children built their houses were given to them by him. Only one child lives in another city and that is because she is a teacher in San José, the capital. A daughter lives with him and she is the one that takes care of him, mainly by cooking.

Bonifacio has always been an independent worker and has freely helped friends all his life with the work they need to do without charge. He was proud to mention that he has always done what he wants and that at present he doesn't have any worries. He said, "I have given my children all of my possessions and I, therefore, don't have anything to worry about. Everything gets solved in this world by God." Happiness for him is being able to visit his friends in the mornings and visiting sick people. His love for horses has always been present in his life and at this point, when he has a pain in any part of his body, he "gets on the horse and goes for a ride and his pains go away."

There is a nice church very close to Bonifacio's house and the land on which the church was built and the flowers planted there were given by him. He is very proud of being from Nicoya and has never moved from the place where he was born. He concluded our interview by asking me if I would marry him.

Summary Observations on Bonifacio's Key Characteristics

- Bonifacio considers one of the secrets to long life is having fun, interacting with others by drinking guaro, a traditional Costa Rican hard liquor, giving and receiving lots of kisses, spending lots of time with groups of friends, dancing often and being very friendly.

- He gets up early every morning and says he visits friends and sick people every day. His loyalty to his father was so strong that he did not get married until his father died.

- Bonifacio's philosophy of life: "Everything in life has solutions. Live happily and in peace, be grateful to God." He feels a strong regional identity, takes medicine whenever he is supposed to, and takes very good care of himself.

29

Francisca Rodríguez Sequeira

101 years old. Carmona, Nandayure

"I had a husband that God had chosen for me."

"I do not live out of sadness; I live out of happiness. My children are excellent, and God is also excellent with me."

One of my first interviews was with Francisca, a 101-year-old lady, who exhibited a number of characteristics that I found over and over again in centenarians that I interviewed. Francisca lives in the small town of Vista del Mar in Carmona, Guanacaste, a district with a total population of 2,500. Once there, we drove around a small soccer field and passed in front of a Catholic church to arrive at a nicely-painted wooden house, where Francisca and her son Luis Ángel Guerrero waited for us. They live in a nice home, which, unlike the homes of most of the centenarians I met, is big and comfortable. Like the other homes, it is very clean. When we arrived at their house just after lunch on a brilliant sunny afternoon, she and her son were sitting on rocking chairs outside on a narrow porch, awaiting our arrival.

Francisca Rodríguez and Dr. Elizabeth Lopez

Foto © Jorge Vindas

Francisca moved to Vista del Mar with her family from a town closer to San José when she was 20 years old because "it had gotten into my father's head that he wanted to move the whole family to be closer to two of his daughters." Francisca's older sisters were married and living in the area. As Francisca reminisced about that time in her life, she had a beautiful sweet smile on her face, and she mentioned that she had a serious relationship with a gentleman then but the relationship ended because of the move. Then she commented, "Life is like this. It was not meant to be that I would marry him." She remembers growing up in a very peaceful environment, saying, "My life was very peaceful as my dad had a farm, he was never rude or harsh with us and the whole family got along together, in the way people at that time used to relate with one another." When she moved to Vista del Mar, the town had only four houses, and was "very boring" for her; it only gradually became the somewhat larger but still small town it is today.

Francisca grew up on a small coffee farm with 11 siblings. She summarized her childhood on the farm by saying, "I cannot complain about anything about my childhood. I played at school and then with friends, and my mother was a very good woman."

Francisca has great memories of her childhood. The family siblings and their friends were like a sisterhood; peaceful and happy. The teachers took them, sometimes just a teacher and her, on outings. As to her time at school, she observed, "There was harmony among everyone — parents, teachers, classmates and friends."

Later on, in this new town, she met the man that would be her husband for 70 years. She told us that he was "the one that God had chosen for me and I thank God that everything came out okay." She feels blessed by God and although she has had two gastric cancer surgeries, "right now she can eat anything."

Francisca has three daughters and a son who have made arrangements together to ensure that at least one will always be available to stay with her, even though according to her, "she doesn't need any assistance for living by herself." The three daughters take turns, one every week, in coming to stay in their mother's home to keep their mother company even though they live in distant cities. The fourth week, the son who lives with her permanently is in charge of providing any assistance that she may need. Although the son lives with her, he has a farm to take care of and cannot, therefore, be available for her if she were to need something except during every fourth week when he doesn't tend the farm and stays with her all day and night.

Francisca feels surrounded by love and never feels lonely as "God gives me everything I need or ask for and it's very rare that he doesn't please me." She says that she lives her life hand in hand with God, and that she has great inner peace. She ended the interview by saying, "I don't live out of sadness — I live out of happiness. My children are excellent, and God is also excellent with me."

She has recently been selected by the community as queen of Nandayure, the local community.

Summary Observations on Francisca's Key Characteristics

- Francisca has a deep faith in God and often expresses gratitude. She accepts life as it comes, holds no grudges, has a positive philosophy of life, and believes that God will provide for everything.

- She feels respected and loved by her children and feels that her authority is respected. She has been endowed with a great memory. Most of her memories are happy memories, her face and sweet smile exude happiness, and she looks forwards to the future.

Saúl
Guzmán Salas

101 years old. Hojancha Centro

"I retired from business
and farming when I was 80 years old."

"I have been very friendly with everyone
all my life and I do not have enemies —
I only have friends."

Saúl Guzmán lives in Hojancha, a charming town in a mountainous region of Nicoya, which is known for its cool, breezy weather. It is the capital of a district of the same name with a population of about 7,500. Hojancha is a lovely town, with the benches around the park painted in different pastel colors and a yellow church right in front of the park. The benches are often full of people conversing with one another and there is a pervasive atmosphere of peace and relaxation all around. Saúl, who is now 101 years old, has lived there for 80 years. When we came to see him, several members of his family came to greet us at the door and invited us to go through the house to the back porch where we found Saúl surrounded by three of his children, their spouses and grandchildren, all sitting in a circle.

Saúl's house is surrounded by his children's houses with constant communication among the houses and grandchildren and adults of all ages coming in and out of his house all the time. Saúl gave a piece of land to each of his children so they could build their homes and live nearby.

Saúl came to Hojancha from a larger town, San Ramón, in his early twenties. Even though he was not born in Hojancha, he has developed a strong regional identity.

He is tall, healthy-looking and friendly. He quickly and easily got fully involved in a lively conversation with us. Like Francisca, he had grown up in a family of eleven siblings. He informed us that "he had grown up in the business world" as his father had a convenience store and meat market that also served as the neighborhood bar. Saúl doesn't remember anything before he was 8 years old, at which time he began working in the family business. He remembers having very few good friends while growing up because he did not consider his classmates to be friends. He considered them classmates and "the only real friend is God, who is the one friend that one can trust."

Saúl worked all his life until he retired a few years ago. At an early age, he would begin working at about 7 or 8 in the morning and would stop at 9 p.m., except on the days he walked for a mile to school. He told us that school was very easy for him.

Saúl liked to go to the town center to watch the girls going by in the afternoons after school before going to work at his father's business. He was already a soccer player then and continued playing until he was 70.

He has worked in several different jobs after stopping work in his father's business when he moved out of the house. He became a policeman for a time and was involved with farming all his life until he retired from business and farming when he was 80 years old.

Saúl is married and has had 11 children. He remembers that every Christmas he would buy a gift for each of the 11 young children to give to their mother. And he proudly told us, "As far as food is concerned, my family never missed having enough food, as they could get everything from the farm I own."

Saúl says he has been a very happy man all his life, never likes to be sad, plays several different musical instruments, and now enjoys listening to Mexican music. He considers Hojancha and Nicoya to be happy places to live "because people like to dance, and marimba music creates a great ambience."

Saúl told us that he liked to have friends but never fully trusted them. Despite this comment and his earlier comments about his classmates, Saúl told us, "I have been very friendly with everyone all my life and I don't have enemies. I only have friends." Whenever he was stressed out or worried, he explained he would call on God for help, asking him to help him from the bottom of his heart.

Saúl now goes to bed at 8 and gets up at 8 in the morning. His diet is usually rice and beans sometimes with some vegetables, and he very much likes almost all kinds of fruit. He likes to have a tortilla with sour cream or a slice of cheese and a cup of coffee for breakfast and he drinks coffee twice a day. His favorite foods are rice, beans, beef and eggs.

Saúl takes very good care of himself and does 400 "circles" where he moves his legs and arms simultaneously on a portable bicycle that he has at home. He does not take any medication, and he says that he has never suffered from a serious illness or serious problems.

Summary Observations on Saúl's Key Characteristics

- He worked very hard in his life as a miner, farmer, policeman and businessman. He is proud of taking very good care of himself and doing 400 rotations every day on a stationary bike where he moves his legs and arms simultaneously.

- Friendships are very important for Saúl even though he does not trust them. He likes being agreeable, avoiding problems, never being sad, and being a pleasant person to be around.

- He and his wife live surrounded by adult children and their families, and three of their children live with them, even though they are grown up.

Estanislao Suárez Suárez

101 years old. Corralillo, Nicoya

"I shared cows and vegetables
and fruit with neighbors."

"I am a happy man
and like to play guitars and dance."

After driving a long time in hot weather on narrow curvy roads, we arrived at the center of the small town of Corralillo which had a traditional Spanish square surrounded by small businesses, a small old-style Catholic church and a few, old wooden houses. As is typical throughout Nicoya, some people were sitting in front of the houses rocking leisurely, just spending time and socializing.

Estanislao's pulpería, an old type of Costa Rican convenience store, has been on the corner across from the square for years selling all kinds of fresh fruit and vegetables, soft drinks, basic food staples, paper and cleaning products. Every piece of furniture in this pulpería is made from dark wood that looks like it has been there forever. There is a desk and a rocking chair behind an L-shaped counter.

When we arrived, Estanislao, the centenarian, was seated in the rocking chair with his feet high up on the desk. He is a tall, slender man, with a face that has recognizable Guanacastecan male features, including a straight nose and bright vivacious eyes, that exude peace and happiness. He was neatly dressed in brown denim pants and a matching brown shirt.

As we entered the pulpería, a middle-aged, friendly-looking woman came out to greet us and invited us to go behind the counter to where her father was seated. Estanislao was looking at us with a questioning expression on his face. I explained to him that we were there to talk to him about his life history and how he had lived to be more than 100 years old. After explaining my purpose in interviewing him for a book I was writing, I asked permission to take some photographs and promised that we would give him a copy of the book once it was published.

He quickly agreed, responded easily to questions, and began to tell us about his life. With a great sense of pride and without much prompting, he shared with us that he has lived in the town since 1949 but has always been an entrepreneur; he has owned a convenience store for 68 years. When he first came to Corralillo, the only way to get there was by oxcart or on horseback. There were no other businesses or shops around.

Estanislao kept talking even without us asking questions, obviously feeling pride in sharing his life history and stories with us. He told us that he cannot ask God for anything else as he has his business, his children, a son and a daughter. He mentioned that his mother did not want him to get married and that's the reason that he didn't until he was 27, when he married an 18-year-old girl. His son comes every night to keep him company, and a daughter spends the day with him while also selling products at the convenience store.

Estanislao is in excellent health, takes very good care of himself, and takes a shower by himself every morning. He has never had a headache in his life. His diet has always been rice, beans, squash and meat. Whenever he killed a cow, he would send part of the meat to his neighbors as well as sending beans when they were harvested. He strongly believes that food was healthier in the old days but now it's full of chemicals, so he prefers produce that is grown locally without much fertilizer or insecticides.

He managed and supervised his small business and personal finances until five years ago. He proudly mentions that he was successful even though many people owed money to his father and when he died no one paid the money back.

There is a bench on the sidewalk outside his pulpería where Estanislao sits every afternoon to converse with people who go by. He is happy, friendly and outgoing and the people in the town like to come and spend time talking with him.

Estanislao believes in God and goes to church often, attending mass every time there is a service in town. He told us, "I do not govern anything. I do not own anything. God and my children take care of me. God is the one that governs everything in my life."

He considers himself a happy man who often used to play guitar and dance. He is very proud of being from Guanacaste and has never considered the idea of moving, telling us, "There is no need to move from place to place. I have always had everything I needed in my life in Corralillo."

Summary Observations
on Estanislao's Key Characteristics

- Estanislao respected parental authority by not marrying until he was 27 as his mother did not want him to get married. It has been very important for him to have lived in the same town for most of his life.

- He has always had his business and practiced a collectivistic approach to sharing what he produces. His lifestyle is very healthy. For example, he sleeps every night from 9 p.m. to 6 a.m.

- Estanislao feels very proud about not owing anything, not doing anything now and having nothing to worry about. He is extremely friendly and happy and often plays the guitar and dances.

Trinidad
Espinoza Medina

101 years old. Quebrada Honda, Nicoya

"I love to have friends, women as well as men,
and these friends come and visit me;
my friends make me happy."

"I love Nicoya and I was born here,
so I will die in this region."

When we arrived, Trinidad was seated on a back porch without walls. The floor inside her home was hardened soil, and the furniture consisted of a wooden bench on one side and a few four-legged wooden stools on the other. Trinidad, who was very friendly, asked us to sit down. She was dressed in a light-blue cotton dress and looked very happy despite her humble surroundings. From within the house, we could easily hear the birds singing all around us, and since there were no walls, there was a breeze that kept the air moving even though it was a hot afternoon.

Trinidad had been informed in advance of our visit and was expecting me to be a medical doctor, so I had to explain to her that I am a well-being psychologist and that my reason for being there was to talk about her life for a book I was writing. I also told her how much I appreciated her kindness in giving me an opportunity to talk to her. She responded with a smile and a very sweet look in her eyes that signaled her approval for me to continue talking to her.

Trinidad began by sharing that when she and her husband had first lived in the house, it had a roof made of dry palm leaves. As time went by, however they were able to change the roof to one made from sand and soil and later to a shake roof. It was in this house that her 12 children were born, five of whom have died. She said it was important that she mention that one of her sons had died recently as she had been very, very sad, had cried a lot and had eaten very little.

In the open-ended conversation that followed, Trinidad mentioned several points relating to her relationship with

God. She prays every night, asking God "not to take her yet as she doesn't want to leave her children alone" (even though they are in their seventies and eighties). These "children" take her in a wheelchair to mass every week, and she prays for world peace and a world free of drugs. She "thanks God because she hasn't lost her mind and for the fact that she has never had to go to bed hungry." She also asks God to help her with her sorrows when she prays as he is the one that heals.

Foto: © Cristina E. Díaz

Trinidad Espinoza Medina

Trinidad has an excellent sense of humor and she loves to laugh. Laughing loudly, she told us, "I went to school for the first time when I was 25 years old and never learned anything." She went on to say that her upbringing was very strict, and her parents did not believe that school was important, so they did not allow her to go to school until that age. She got married at 30 to a man that she chose but she has been a widow for 25 years. She said it was a very good marriage and they worked together, had 12 children and lived on the plantains, corn, rice, beans, pork and poultry their small farm produced. They also ate beef and fish regularly.

Trinidad loves to dance, and even now at 101, she likes to be wheeled by her children to dances where she takes great pride in paying for her own ticket. She loves to see the people dancing, and she told us, "My spirit gets happy when I listen to happy music." When I asked about her friends, Trinidad answered that she loves to have friends, women as well as men, and that when these friends come to visit her, it makes her very happy. They bring her gifts and food and she also gives them food. She mentioned that when she is sad, she sits on the porch to wait for one or two friends to come by and talk to her and make her happy.

Trinidad shared a story with us about the time her husband went to sell their farm produce at the market but returned home without any money. From then on, she said, she was the one who went to sell their produce in the market. She also told us that when she and her husband were young, they would go to parties and dance, and if he got drunk, she would come back home by herself. Trinidad certainly seems to be a very strong and determined woman.

Trinidad is very proud to be from Nicoya and ended our conversation by saying, "I think that since I was born in Nicoya, I will die here."

Summary Observations on Trinidad's Key Characteristics

- Trinidad is a remarkable, happy centenarian. She is a dancer and partygoer who needs to see people to be happy. Her friends visit her almost every day and bring her food.

- Trust and faith in God are everything for Trinidad.

- She has a strong sense of personal and regional identity and did the same jobs men did when she was younger.

53

Romualdo
Álvarez Álvarez

105 years old. 27 de Abril, Santa Cruz

"I have loved friends since childhood
and love to party, especially if there are guitars,
marimbas and dancing."

"I worked since I finished attending school
after 3rd grade and until I retired."

Jorge and I accepted an invitation to Romualdo's 105th birthday celebration. When we arrived on a Sunday afternoon, we noticed that about 25 people had already gathered for the party on a dry grassless patio. It was, however, a very pleasant spot, as it was a warm, breezy day, and we were all seated under the shadow of big trees, surrounded by singing birds accompanied by very noisy parakeets.

The group of invitees was made up of relatives and friends of all ages (from 4 years old up). It was a family-oriented atmosphere, but there were a number of friends, including, of course, the prerequisite guitar player. The centenarian's daughter, her partner Quintín and Romualdo were without a doubt among the happiest people in the group.

The celebration went on for about three hours during which the guests were served arroz de maíz (a corn dish made to look like rice), natural fruit drinks, no alcohol and a birthday cake that we had brought as a gift. It was a joyful and memorable celebration complete with numerous songs and toasts for Romualdo and his well-being.

We returned to the house a week later to speak with Romualdo who was with his daughter and his son-in-law, Quintín, as both live with him, take care of him, and help him get around as he can no longer get around by himself.

It was around 9 in the morning when we arrived at his house, and he was waiting for us on the same patio where the celebration had taken place. Romualdo had already taken a shower, eaten breakfast, and was dressed in nice clean, well-pressed clothes. In a cheerful and proud voice, he shared that he likes to take a shower every day and that he does that by himself. He began to share his life history with us by telling us that he only went to school for three years and that he had been worked from them until he retired at the age of 90. He remembered getting a machete as a gift when he was 8 and that at that age he would go to the field with the older workers. He would give his parents all the money he made, and they, in turn, would buy him what he needed. His father had many partners and his mother also had several partners. He was one of 21 children all of whom worked together to help the parents grow corn and beans, but not other crops like lettuce, radishes and tomatoes "because no one knew about them." They would eat what the farm produced, and they would also eat beef.

As a child, Romualdo would walk to school barefoot on the muddy roads, as there was no money for shoes — so he and the other children would rinse their feet before going into the classroom. He told us he has been very peaceful all his life and this has resulted in his having many friends. He has always liked to listen to music and dance while enjoying his peaceful life. Since Romualdo was a child, he has enjoyed having friends and has loved to party, especially if there were guitars and marimbas.

Romualdo married at 35 and his reason for waiting so long was that many times he had to work away from home and could only come home for Holy Week and Christmas. He has worked all his life from 6 a.m. to 7 p.m. except Sundays.

Many times, he did not even have a horse to ride to work so he would have to walk long distances to get there. Once he got married, he settled down in a house right across from where he lives now.

He remembers that at the age of 60, he was very happy with his life, and as he had always taken very good care of himself, he thought he would like to continue to live for a long time even though he wished he could be younger so he could continue to work as he always had. He also feels bad that he can no longer produce the rice, beans and other food that his daughter and Quintín eat.

Romualdo has been a strong believer in God, telling us, "God is the one that governs everything and no one has power except him." He prays to God for help with his life and used to pray for help with his work.

He also told us that for 57 years he has been a *mayordomo* with responsibility for taking care of St. Esquipulas and making sure that every house that the saint would visit was appropriate and ready to welcome him.

He said that he has been very generous his whole life, giving lots of love and material possessions to others. He ended our conversation by saying, "Whatever would come to me I would give it to other people."

Summary Observations on Romualdo's Key Characteristics

- Romualdo was one of 21 children with a somewhat chaotic family life. His father had many partners and his mother also had several partners. He worked from the age of 9, and his parents would take all the money he made.

- He strongly believes that no one has power except God, and he accepts his physical reality of not walking well without getting sad or angry because it is God's will. He says he has always been a happy man.

- Romualdo takes great pride in being from Guanacaste and in being generous.

Dimas
Sequeira Sequeira

103 years old. Mansión, Nicoya

"I have seldom had to take even an aspirin."

"At 6 years of age,
I was selling what older women would sell."

Dimas' house, at the end of a long driveway some 300 yards long, is modern, with a big combined living/dining room and lots of windows that allow the air to flow freely. Upon arrival, we were greeted by one of Dimas' two daughters, a friendly woman, full of vitality and in her seventies. She lives with Dimas while the other daughter, who lives in New Jersey, comes to spend the winters in Costa Rica. The daughters take turns taking care of her.

Dimas is a petite, thin lady, full of laughter and friendly smiles with a fantastic memory. Indeed, she can remember Costa Rican songs from her childhood, and recalls detailed geographical features of Costa Rica. She proudly demonstrated this by laughingly reciting for us the questions she had been asked on a third-grade geography test.

Dimas took great pride in telling us that she had been an entrepreneur since she was 6 years old. She told us, "I grew up doing things that older women used to do; however, at that time I was a young girl, it was lots of fun." She always loved to make things that she could sell and vividly remembered being eight years old and rushing to get food ready to be sold, some of it to groups of her friends.

Dimas worked very hard all her life, getting up at 3 a.m. when she worked and, when she was younger, leaving the house at 6 a.m. to walk one hour to school and walking one hour back in the afternoon. She spent all her life working hard as she and her husband owned a farm. She planted and harvested rice and other produce, and cooked to feed the workers, sometimes up to 15 of them. At the same time, she was doing all the housework and taking care of 12 children.

She raised pigs for sale while she was attending school, and remembered that at 25 she would bake corn pastries, which she would place in a big bowl on her head and then go out to sell them. Sometimes, she would ride a horse for 12 hours to get to a town where she sold her products, and she laughingly told us that on those rides, she "was like a monkey grabbing the box of pastries,"; however, she "never fell down from the horse." Dimas also bought and sold cattle and even bought a farm and the very nice house in which they live, all with her own money.

Dimas married at 32 and had the first of her 12 children at the age of 34. She told us she took very good care of herself throughout her life, so her health has been excellent, and she has seldom needed to even take an aspirin. Whenever she has had to take medication, she has carefully done so exactly as indicated. She was still able to take a shower by herself but had some difficulty walking. Dimas has always been very social and greatly enjoyed visits to her house from relatives or friends. She mentioned that she particularly valued these visits now that she was not strong enough to go out to visit them.

Dimas had strong pride in her Nicoyan identity and told us Nicoya had everything one may need as well as work for everyone that wants to work.

I will always have fond memories of my conversation with Dimas, her smile, sense of humor, business sense, love for people and her kindness toward Jorge and me while we were interviewing her.

Dimas Sequiera and Jorge Vindas

Summary Observations on Dimas' Key Characteristics

- Dimas' memory is extraordinarily good, and even now, she can remember third-grade quiz questions. She also has an excellent sense of humor.

- She has been extremely hardworking ever since she was a little girl. As an adult, she was a very capable business woman and her entrepreneurial spirit helped her succeed in life.

Pablo
Castillo Carrillo

95 years old. Mansión, Nicoya

"There is nothing more beautiful in life
than friendship."

"I would like to be buried with mariachis."

While Pablo is only 95, we interviewed him because he is the son of a famous centenarian named Panchita Castillo, who died last year at 110 years old. When we arrived at his humble home, all the windows and doors were closed even though it was very hot and the humidity was low. We had to go around to the back of the house where we found him lying in a hammock under a mango tree. The backyard was hard soil without grass or any plants other than the tree. This fellow was barefoot and dressed in simple knee-high trousers and a plaid shirt.

Pablo lives by himself in small quarters consisting of one small room and a kitchen that are part of a bigger house. He told us that he lives alone and in peace; no one bothers him and he cannot bother anyone. He is proud that he lives very happily with little money (while eating very healthy food) and with nothing to worry about. He never married because the first girl he proposed to said, "No."

He gets up every morning at 5 a.m. and walks to visit friends who live in the neighborhood, a pastime he very much enjoys. He told us, "There is nothing more beautiful in life than friendships," and friends are a very important factor in his life. Pablo has been an avid dancer, and he loves mariachis and marimbas to the point that he said to us, "I would like to be buried with mariachis."

Although he worked hard for many years, at this point in his life, he doesn't work at all, spending his life socializing and sitting in the shade of the big tree behind his house.

While his diet is made up primarily of beans, rice and meat, he told us his mother and grandmother taught him to eat everything. Like virtually all the centenarians, Pablo is deeply religious and prays every night "as God forbids that he does not do so."

Pablo Castillo

Foto: © Cristina E. Díaz

Summary Observations on Pablo's Key Characteristics

- Pablo is extremely happy and friendly. He likes to please other people. He makes a round of visits to his friends by 7 a.m. every morning. He likes to find solutions if there are problems.

- He has a strong belief in God, and says God forbids him from not praying every night. He would like to be "buried with mariachis."

- Pablo strongly identifies with the Nicoya Peninsula and its culture, stating proudly that he never abandoned his place in Matina and eats every local food just as he was taught by his mother and grandmother.

The following two interviews
are with two people who
are experts on Nicoya's centenarians:
José Carlos Moraga,
a local school teacher, and last,
but certainly not least,
my research assistant,
Jorge Vindas.

José Carlos
Moraga Gutiérrez

Santa Cruz, Nicoya. High-School Teacher

"Always present was the concept of the family
as a unit of collaboration, and values were taught
through the group."

"Grandpa talked about respect for oneself,
respect for others, solidarity and group unity."

Romualdo Álvarez and José Carlos Moraga

José Carlos Moraga, the great-nephew of a centenarian (Romualdo Álvarez) is a high-school teacher in Santa Cruz, Nicoya. I requested an interview with him after hearing a remarkably eloquent toast he made at his great-uncle's 105th birthday party. I was interested in interviewing him as he had given me the impression of being knowledgeable and immersed in the Nicoyan culture, having lived there all his life. I was particularly interested in hearing his views on the relationship between elders and the younger generations.

We met at an outdoor cafe in Santa Cruz, Nicoya where we sat at a narrow table directly on the sidewalk. It was 4 o'clock in the afternoon and there were many people passing by on the street, shopping, socializing, trying to get back home after work, or just out walking.

José Carlos told me that while attending college, he looked forward to his regular visits to see his elderly grandfather, who he described as full of life, vitality and wisdom, and to listen to him talk about respect for oneself, respect for others, solidarity and group unity. He also talked about their mutual payment system in which people would often not get paid for the work they did for others but would receive free help from those same people when they needed it. It was also a system within which people who worked on a farm would not get paid until the crop was sold but would be paid at that time. This was how reciprocity worked in Nicoya's collectivistic society.

He told me that when he was growing up, values were taught through the group, and the family was viewed as a unit of collaboration. For José Carlos, "Grandpa taught us about work values, not only teaching the immediate family, but also other relatives and even the godchildren."

Moneywise, Grandpa helped everyone who needed it. José Carlos, even today, can still hear his grandfather saying, "Always buy with cash, and if someone gives you a hand, do not ask for his elbow."

Summary Observations on José Carlos' Comments

- José Carlos knows that his identity was shaped by the way he was brought up and by the elders whom he grew up with. It is obvious that in Nicoyan culture there is great respect for elders, and, for José Carlos, elders transmit mutual respect as well as other moral values, not only to him but to the whole family and friends. The obvious respect shown toward elders and their ideas gives them support for their healthy self-esteem.

Jorge Vindas López

Blue Zones Research Assistant and
an expert on Nicoya's centenarians

"Talking to a centenarian is as fascinating
as reading a great book you can't stop reading."

"Centenarians were very obedient
to their parents' requests.
Their children respect their parents' wishes
no matter how old the parents are now."

Jorge has dedicated the last 15 years of his life to working with the centenarians living in the Guanacaste area, particularly the Nicoya Peninsula. He has visited all their homes, many on a regular basis. He has become close friends with virtually all the centenarians and their families, and has spent endless hours speaking to them, getting to know as much as possible about them and their lives — how they grew up and even when their birthdays are. His knowledge of Nicoya's centenarians is based on in-depth, first-hand experience. Naturally, therefore, I continued my quest to understand the lessons to be learned from how Costa Rica's centenarians live to be 100 by asking Jorge to summarize what he has learned over the years about how they did it.

Gregoria Hernández and Jorge Vindas

He told me there were many lessons he had learned from the centenarians about what they have done or who they are that have resulted in their remarkable longevity. Here are some of those lessons.

Eight lessons from the centenarians

1. Have a relaxed lifestyle and enjoy life. They are happy, live in the now, and are stress-free.

2. Take good care of yourself physically.

3. Be good, kind people who share with others. Centenarians have been very generous throughout their lives.

4. Respect yourself in every way. For example, the centenarians have always respected the need to take the time to take a siesta after lunch and most nap at different times during the day.

5. Be very obedient to your parents' requests. Children respect their parents' wishes no matter how old the parents are.

6. Do not buy things you cannot afford. They avoid complexities and stressors, financially and otherwise.

7. Have a simple lifestyle, living with the basics, with little more than a piece of land, a roof over your head and food to eat.

8. Live in peace with much happiness. The centenarians are happy people.

5

Yes! Culture and Personality Can Increase Longevity

The seven summarized Nicoya centenarian life-history portraits presented in this book display a highly-consistent interweaving of life experiences, cultural factors and personality characteristics. They have helped these interesting, fascinating and, in their own way, wise human beings achieve a much longer life than most other people, even those with access to far better economic and medical support and far better access to information on the benefits of nutrition, exercise, rest and reduction of stress. How have they done that?

Other analysis of Nicoya's centenarians, especially Dan Buettner's excellent book on the blue zones, has provided extremely-valuable insights into the role that diet and exercise play. There has, however, been far less analysis of the significant contributions of culture and personality to longevity. The perspectives shared by the seven centenarians and one 95-year-old son, (representing more than 800 years of life experience), as well as by other professionals I interviewed, provide valuable additional insight into how individuals who wish to live a younger, healthier and happier life can change attitudes and behavior to improve the probability of achieving a life goal of living happily for more than 100 years.

These insights into attitudes and behaviors that contribute to greater longevity can be grouped within four main areas of influence: i) cultural factors; ii) personality traits and behaviors driven from within a person; iii) lifestyle; and iv) other key factors. The centenarians made many statements during the interviews, some of which are listed as quotes in Appendix 2, that give evidence supporting the key role of these factors in their lives.

Influence of Culture

Four key cultural factors that play an important role in increasing centenarians' longevity include the collectivistic culture in which they live, the Pura Vida culture, deep respect for the elderly, and having deep roots in and a sense of identification with the place they live.

In Costa Rica's collectivistic society, the human support network, which can be defined as family, friends and to some extent the community, has a primary role in approving and influencing each individual's behavior. In an individualistic culture, such as that in the U.S., individuals have that primary responsibility for themselves. Typical conversations at parties in countries where two people are getting to know each other illustrate the difference in how people are viewed in individualistic and collectivistic societies. In individualistic societies, one of the first questions often asked to identify better the person one is meeting for the first time is "What do you do?" (i.e. "What is your work?"). In a collectivistic society, that first question asked is far more likely to be "Who are you related to?" or "Who do you know?" All the centenarians in this study have lived all their lives in a collectivistic society. Here are some comments that support this.

> "Always present was the concept of the family as a unit of collaboration and values were taught through the group." – José Carlos Moraga

> "I get up at a 5 a.m. and start walking and visiting friends." – Pablo Castillo

Foto: © Jorge Vindas

Jose Carlos Moraga, Tropical Biologist and Dr. Elizabeth Lopez

> "I shared cows and vegetables and fruit with neighbors." — Estanislao Suárez

> "Grandpa talked about respect for oneself, respect for others, solidarity and group unity." — José Carlos Moraga

Family and friendships play a more important role in a collectivistic society than they do in an individualistic society. Virtually every interviewee stressed the great importance of family and friends throughout their lifetimes, from childhood to adulthood to elderescence[16] to old age. Friendships have a pervasive impact on their happiness, feelings of well-being, and self-esteem. All of them gather often with groups of friends to have parties, celebrate important occasions, or simply to visit in the late afternoon.

> "Happiness for me is to be with friends." — José Bonifacio Villegas

> "All my life, I have liked friends, liked to dance, listen to music, and enjoyed a peaceful life." — Romualdo Álvarez Álvarez

---

16 Elderescence is a new term that has come into vogue as people now live longer. It describes that period after people stop working, often 65 or 70 for most people, until the time when true physical old age sets in, usually in the mid to late eighties (possibly in the nineties in the case of many of Nicoya's centenarians).

> "I enjoy when relatives and friends come to visit me." — Dimas Sequeira Sequeira

In a collectivistic society, there is usually great respect for elders, and the centenarians interviewed feel very much respected by their children, grandchildren, great grandchildren, neighbors and friends. This mutual respect continuously validates the centenarians' existence and their view of their role in the family as important. This validation enhances their self-esteem and can help them continue to feel they have a purpose, no matter how physically frail they may be. These centenarians regularly transmit traditions, values and beliefs to younger generations by close interaction with them, as can be seen in the following quotes.

> "Grandpa taught all of us about work values, not only the immediate family but also the godchildren and other relatives." — José Carlos Moraga

> "I have for many years lived surrounded by my adult children; three adult children still live with me." — Sául Guzmán

> "Centenarians were very obedient to their parents' requests. Their children respect their parents' wishes no matter how old the parents are now." — Jorge Vindas López

The centenarians respected parental authority when they were growing up, even to the point of not getting married if a parent did not want them to as well as their references to living with parents if they were needed regardless of age. Several centenarians commented on this.

> "I could not leave father until his death, when I was 28 years old." – José Bonifacio Villegas

> "I only married at 27 years of age because my mother did not want me to get married." – Estanislao Suárez

Like most Costa Ricans, these centenarians practice and live Pura Vida (Pure Life), a phrase one hears repeated over and over again virtually every day in Costa Rica. It is a way of life, even a philosophy, that carries with it the idea of enjoying life and being happy. It tends to be present-oriented and somewhat carefree, reducing the importance of time, taking away time pressure, and reducing the need to worry or plan. Pura Vida is also an uncluttered lifestyle that includes a deep appreciation for family and friends, nature and peace. These centenarians practice and love peace and value a peaceful existence.

> "I do not live out of sadness, I live out of happiness; my children are excellent, and God is also excellent with me." – Francisca Rodríguez Sequeira

Francisca Rodríguez

Foto: © Jorge Vindas

"Centenarians have a simple lifestyle, live with the basics, and have a piece of land, a roof over their head and food to eat." – Jorge Vindas

The lives of most of the centenarians I interviewed are filled with partying, music and dancing with friends, a widespread

Guanacastecan tradition. There were many references to that.

> "I have loved friends since childhood and love to party, especially if there are guitars, marimbas and dancing." – Romualdo Álvarez Álvarez

> "I would like to be buried with mariachis." – Pablo Castillo Carrillo

> "I am a happy man and like to play guitars and dance." – Estanislao Suárez Suárez

Finally, most of the centenarians never left Nicoya and they have a strong sense of belonging and of personal and regional identity (i.e. knowing who they are and who their family and friends are).

> "I love Nicoya and I was born here, so I will die in this region." – Trinidad Espinoza

> "My identity was shaped by the way I was brought up, and the people I grew up with." – José Carlos Moraga

Influence of Personality Traits and Behaviors

Personality traits make a significant contribution to increasing longevity and, like culture, should be considered a

Pablo Castillo in his backyard

causative factor in addition to genetic, physical, biological and lifestyle factors in achieving a long, healthy and happy life.

Belief in God, which is both a cultural and personality attribute, is paramount to their existence. Most of them practice Catholicism, pray regularly, attend mass, and participate in religion. The belief that God is responsible for everything and helps to solve problems catalyzes a fatalistic attitude that allows centenarians to relieve stress "as God will provide." In believing this, they exhibit a personality characteristic that can reduce stress called 'external locus of control.' [17]

All the interviewed centenarians are deeply religious, and many referred to being protected by God. Their religious views are very concrete and often fatalistic as many believe their future will be whatever God has planned for them. This may play a key role in reducing stress which in turn enhances longevity. While these centenarians are conscientious about taking good care of themselves, they often express little concern about dealing with the problems in their lives. Many believe God will take care of them. This was powerfully brought home to me during my earlier Blue Zones™ expedition when I concluded a conversation with Abuela Panchita, then 102 years old, by giving her 10,000 colones (the equivalent of about $20) because I felt sorry for her. Abuela Panchita reacted by clapping her hands with joy and telling me, "I knew it, I knew it! This morning I woke up with no money to buy food but I knew that God would provide."

> "God governs everything and no one and nothing has power over Him."
>
> Romualdo Álvarez

---

17 External locus control is a belief that something external, in this case God, is in control of one's life.

"I do not govern anything I do and do not own anything; God and my children are in charge of me and God is the one that governs everything."

Estanislao Suárez Suárez

"God gives me everything I need or ask for and it's very rare that he does not please me."

Francisca Rodríguez Sequeira

Finally, in a surrounding environment of happiness,[18] the Nicoyan centenarians exude happiness, and it is at the core of their existence. As Douglas Smith states in his book "People who are happy can return to this core again and again, even in times of turmoil and adversity." In addition to being happy, all the centenarians interviewed laughed,[19] many of them often, and they have an excellent spontaneous sense of humor.

18 Several studies have named Costa Rica as one of the happiest countries in the world. In *The Blue Zones of Happiness: Lessons from the World's Happiest People*, Dan Buettner writes a whole chapter on Costa Rica that includes the following comment — "Generally speaking the richer a country is, the happier it is. But this effect is most pronounced among nations that are struggling just to provide basic needs. Costa Rica goes beyond that, producing the highest day-to-day happiness, the largest number of happy life-years (the sum of life expectancy and life satisfaction) and one of the world's lowest rates of middle-age mortality delivers more happiness per GDP dollar than anywhere else."

19 In the book, *Laugh*, Lisa Sturge lists a number of beneficial physical and psychological benefits to laughter, among which is inhibiting the production of stress hormones in the body, such as cortisol and epinephrine.

Foto: © Cristina E. Díaz

Francisca Rodríguez

"I love to dance, and my spirits get high when I listen to happy music." — Trinidad Espinoza Medina

"They live in peace and very happily. The centenarians are happy people." — Jorge Vindas

"I have always liked to dance and be happy." — José Bonifacio Villegas

In the interviews, these men and women who are more than 100 years old said many things that suggested a predominance of optimistic thinking, positive emotions, agreeableness, openness and generosity, not only towards their immediate family, but also with friends, neighbors and the community. Moreover, virtually nothing was said that suggested symptoms of anxiety, depression or even feeling vulnerable.

> "I do not live out of sadness I live out of happiness; my children are excellent, and God is also excellent with me." – Francisca Rodríguez Sequeira

> "Grandpa would help anyone that was needing money." – José Carlos Moraga

The centenarians also displayed traits of self-discipline that would impact how well they take care of themselves by taking medicines, having a good diet, and physically protecting themselves. Emotional competence seems to be the norm. These traits can be grouped in psychology under the term 'conscientiousness'.

> "I learned to take care of myself since I was very young." – Pablo Castillo Carrillo

"I take very good care of myself and do 400 circles daily in a bike where I move my legs and arms simultaneously." – Saúl Guzmán Salas

The Influence of Lifestyle

While this book is not primarily about lifestyle, especially as it relates to diet and exercise, both are extremely important factors in increasing the Nicoyan centenarians' longevity.

Nicoya's centenarians have a simple but healthy diet. While far less diversified than the diet in wealthier places, it uses locally produced foodstuffs in innovative and effectively diversified ways to promote health and long life. It includes many innovative meals that are imaginatively created. They are based mainly on beans, rice, corn, squash, chayote, some meat, poultry and fish, fresh fruit, coffee and water. Perhaps, the most famous is gallo pinto, literally translated as 'spotted rooster', which is a relatively simple dish made of rice and black beans that may be served at any meal. A few traditional Nicoyan recipes that typify the kind of dishes often eaten by these centenarians can be found in an appendix to this book.

All of the centenarians exercised regularly, often extensively as part of their everyday activities, until the end of elderescence, indeed sometimes into their nineties.

They all worked very hard for most of their lives, usually hard physical work outside in the fields. They would often walk for an hour or more to begin work at 6 a.m., finish in the mid-afternoon and walk back home. While relaxing, they also often exercised while engaged in dancing, the most popular national sport. Probably because of this exercise, most of the centenarians I interviewed were in surprisingly good physical and mental condition. Even their memories were better than I would have expected for people who were more than 100 years old, indeed better than some members of my own generation.

> "I used to ride a horse for 12 hours to take things to be sold." – Dimas Sequeira Sequeira

> "I began working at an early age from seven or eight in the morning and would stop at 9 p.m., except on days when I walked a mile to school. I worked all my life until I retired a few years ago when I was 80." – Saúl Guzmán Salas

> "I managed and supervised my business and personal finances until I was 90." – Estanislao Suárez Suárez

The Influence of Two Other Factors on Longevity

Close Social and Support Networks

The Harvard Grant and Glueck Study tracked the physical and emotional well-being of a group of males and females over a period of 75 years and came to a clear conclusion, according to Robert Waldinger[20]: "The clearest message that we get from this 75-year study is this: *Good relationships keep us happier and healthier.*" The article also mentions that the biggest predictor of your happiness and fulfillment overall in life is, basically, love. "It's not just the number of friends you have or whether or not you are in a committed relationship," says Waldinger, "it's the quality of your close relationships that matters."

My own earlier study of psychological characteristics associated with Costa Rica's centenarians, conducted as part of the 2007 Blue Zones™ expedition, identified close social and support networks with family and friends as a key factor contributing to their longevity. This conclusion was also fully supported by the Nicoyan centenarians interviewed for this book as they all have close relationships and regular interaction with family, friends and usually with the communities in which they live. Having a "significant other," whether a partner or someone else, hugely enriches the social and support network for most of these centenarians.

---

20   Robert Waldinger, Director of the Harvard Study of Adult Development

Time published an article in its July 25, 2016 issue on the healing power of nature stating that there is a large body of evidence to support the idea that "spending time in nature is responsible for measurable beneficial changes in the body." According to Japanese scientists, trees and plants produce aromatic compounds called phytoncides which, when inhaled, can produce healthy biological changes in the body similar to aromatherapy. Spending time in nature can lower one's blood pressure, increase feeling of awe and inspiration, promote cancer-fighting cells, and help with depression, anxiety or ADHD symptoms. Several studies have shown that having a window view of a natural setting can improve attention, reduce stress and speed up recovery from surgeries.

The centenarians in Nicoya, far beyond having only a "window view," are fully surrounded much of the time by nature as their houses have windows that are almost always open to singing birds and green surroundings that give them the opportunity to derive the benefits that trees and other plants can offer. They have also spent much of their time outdoors and in the sun, both earlier in their lives when they worked and now. Time in the sun is known to facilitate production of vitamin D3 which, in turn, maintains strong bones.

It's Up to You

The centenarians have shared important secrets on how they have lived happily to be a still vigorous 100 or more by willingly, indeed enthusiastically, sharing with Jorge and me their life stories and displaying their culture and personalities, (i.e. attributes and behaviors), that have helped lead them to be as old as they are. It is important that we all understand that a wonderful and amazing characteristic of these behaviors is that many of them can be learned and practiced by all of us; we can, if we so desire, make changes in our everyday lives that can improve our ability to live longer, more happily and in a more youthful way.

IT'S UP TO YOU!

Acknowledgements

My special thanks to Paul Murgatroyd, my husband of 20 years, for his constant encouragement and support for writing this book, the initial editing, as well as for adding several valuable insights. From the day we were married, he has provided unwavering support for my professional activities and intellectual endeavors.

Many thanks also to my daughters, Roxana, Cynthia, Gloriana and Sylvia, for understanding their mother and for providing me with unconditional love and support, which have provided a sound foundation for moving forward throughout my life.

I would like to acknowledge specifically the principal actors in this book, the centenarians — Romualdo Álvarez Álvarez, Pablo Castillo Carrillo, Trinidad Espinoza Medina, Saúl Guzmán Salas, Francisca Rodríguez Sequeira, Dimas Sequeira Sequeira, Estanislao Suárez Suárez and José Bonifacio Villegas Fonseca. This book would not have existed without their collaboration and willingness to share their life experiences, and their beliefs, feelings, personality and culture.

My deepest thanks to Dan Buettner, owner and director of Blue Zones LLC, for allowing me to be part of the first expedition to identify the blue zone in Nicoya and discover many of the reasons for the remarkable longevity there. His passion and commitment to longevity and happiness research and his commitment to developing and implementing Blue Zones™ programs with a public-health orientation in different cities, as well as his bestseller books on these topics have been a primary motivator for me to do research on the impact of personality and culture on longevity.

Special thanks to Lillianne Ruiz for her professional interest, effort and commitment in painting the illustration of dancers.

Thanks to Floria Herrero Pinto not only for her friendship over many years but also for her very helpful insights and sharing from her extensive experience as a writer and photographer.

My friend Dwight Hartley deserves a heartfelt acknowledgement for encouraging me to write this book. His efforts in developing food products that can improve health in Costa Rica and the United States have also been a motivating force.

I could not have chosen a better research assistant for this project than Jorge Vindas as he has remarkable skills in making things happen by using his ample knowledge of the Nicoya Peninsula, the centenarians and their families. He arranged all my interviews with the centenarians and their families as well as visits to the Mercado de Nicoa, Hojancha Older Adult Center (facilitated by its director, Soleida Bogantes Porras) and restaurants. He also supplied transportation for each journey. There I met with owners, managers and Juan Carlos Moraga, whose insightful comments on the culture of the Nicoya Peninsula as well as his observations on the personalities of Nicoyans were invaluable.

Finally, I would like to thank six people who were particularly helpful in the preparation of this book, namely Roger Pardo, who helped me design the format, José Gabriel Vindas, whose sophisticated computer skills assisted in solving many technical issues along the way, Tom Zabel for his collaboration in picture selection, Andrea Mickus for her excellent proofreading, Priscilla Coto, who made key contributions to book and picture design, and Inder Sud for his help in preparing its digitization.

Foto: © Jorge Vindas

Bougainvillea

Bibliography

Arauz, C. (2006). *Guanacaste Life and Culture.* San José, Costa Rica: Carlos Arauz Ramos.

Ben-Shahar, T. (2007). *Happier.* United States of America: McGraw-Hill.

Buettner, D. (2008). *The Blue Zone, Lessons for living longer from the people who've lived the longest.* U.S.A: National Geographic Society.

Buettner, D. (2013). *The Blue Zones Solution, Eating and Living like the World's Healthiest People.* Washington, D.C.: National Geographic Society.

Buettner, D. (2017). *The Blue Zones of Happiness, Lessons from the World's Happiest People.* Washington, D.C.: National Geographic Partners.

Buettner, D. (2017, November). *The Search for Happiness.* National Geographic, 30-45.

Curtin, M. (2017). This 75-year Harvard study found the 1 secret to leading a fulfilling life. *Inc*. Retrieved from: https://www.inc.com/melanie-curtin/want-a-life-of-fulfillment-a-75-year-harvard-study-says-to-prioritize-this-one-t.html

DifferenceBetween.com, *Difference Between Attribution Theory and Locus of Control.* (2014, December 3). Retrieved from http://www.differencebetween.com/difference-between-attribution-theory-and-vs-locus-of-control/

Erikson, E. H. (1968). *Identity: Youth and crisis.* New York: W. W. Norton and Company, Inc.

Erikson, E. H. (1980). *Identity and the life of cycle.* New York: W. W. Norton and Company, Inc.

Erikson, E., Erikson, J., & Kivnick, Helen. (1986). *Vital Involvement in Old Age.* U.S.A.: W. W. Norton and Company, Inc.

Esfahani, E. (2017). *The Power of Meaning, Crafting a Life That Matters.* New York: Crown.

García, M & García L. (1986). *Comidas y Bebidas Típicas de Guanacaste.* San José, C.R.: Editorial Costa Rica.

Masui, Y., Gondo, Y., Inagaki, H. & Hirose, N. (2006). Do personality characteristics predict longevity? Findings from the Tokyo Centenarian Study. *Springer.* Retrieved from https://www.ncbi.nlm.nih.gov/pmc/articles/PMC3259156/

Núñez, R. & Marín, J. (2009). *Historia de la (Re)Construcción de una Región.* 1850-2007. San José, C.R.: Alma Mater.

Núñez, R. & Rodríguez, A. (2016). *Guanacaste: Región e Historia 1786-2015.* San José, C.R.: Alma Mater.

Rodin, J. (2014). *The Resilience Dividend.* U.S.A.: Public Affairs.

Rotter, J. B. (1975). Some problems and misconceptions related to the construct of internal versus external control of reinforcement. *Journal of Counseling and Clinical Psychology,* 43 (1), 56-67.

Rotter, J. B. (1966). Generalized expectancies for internal versus external control of reinforcement. *Psychological Monographs: General and Applied,* 80 (1).

Rotter, S. M., & Liverant, S. (1962). Internal versus external control of reinforcement: A major variable in behavior theory. In N. F. Washburn (Ed.), *Decisions, values and groups*: Vol II. London: Pergaman.

Salas, I., Camacho, F. & Guier, I. (2014). *Huellas de Nuestra Raíz Chorotega: Recorrido histórico de los primeros pobladores en la Gran Nicoya (2000 a.C. - 1550 d.C.)*. San José, C.R.: Masterlitho.

Sancho, E. & Baraona, M. (2007). *Frutas Tropicales de Costa Rica. San José, C.R.: Zona Tropical*

Seligman, M. (2002). *Authentic Happiness*. New York, NY: Free Press.

Seligman, M. (2006). *Learned Optimism, How to Change Your Mind and Your Life*. U.S.A.: Vintage Books.

Sifferlin, A. (2016, July). *The Healing Power of Nature. Time*, 23-26.

Smith, D. (2014). *Happiness, The Art of Living with Peace, Confidence and Joy*. Columbus, OH: White Pine Mountain.

Sturge, L. *Laugh*. (2017, May). London, UK: Quadrille

Thayer, J. & Thayer, P. (2005). *Elderescence, The Gift of Longevity*. Lanham, MD: Hamilton Books.

Waterman, A.S. (1982). Identity development from adolescence to adulthood: An extension of theory and a review of research. *Developmental Psychology*, 18 (3), 341-358.

Waterman, A.S. (1984). *The psychology of individualism*. New York: Praeger.

Recipes

This appendix provides recipes for a selective few of the many typical dishes that Nicoya's centenarians have eaten often over the years. These recipes have been contributed by María José Guido Obando, Gioconda Rangel, Carmen Viquez, the ladies working at the Nicoa Market and the director and participants in the Hojancha Older Adults Center. My heartfelt thanks to all of them.

Salads

Etelvina's Cabbage Salad

INGREDIENTS

- 1 small shredded cabbage
- ½ cup shredded carrots
- ¼ cup chopped cilantro
- The juice of ½ a lemon
- 1 diced tomato
- Olive oil, pepper and salt to taste

PREPARATION:

1. Have all the ingredients ready ahead of time and mix at time of serving.

Potato Salad with Carrots

INGREDIENTS

- 2 lb peeled, cooked and diced potatoes
- 1 lb cooked and diced carrots
- 1 cup mayonnaise
- ½ cup ketchup
- Olive oil (optional)
- Dash of salt (optional)

PREPARATION:

1. Mix potatoes, carrots, mayonnaise, ketchup and olive oil.

2. Refrigerate for at least 5 hours.

3. Decorate with parsley and serve.

Green and Red Cabbage Salad

- 1 small green cabbage
- 1 small red cabbage
- 1 cup carrots
- ½ cup pineapple juice
- ¼ cup apple cider vinegar
- 1 tbsp sugar
- Dash of salt

PREPARATION:

1. Shred the green and red cabbages, mix with shredded carrots, pineapple juice, vinegar, salt and sugar.

2. Prepare 30 minutes before serving.

Main Dishes

Marinated Beef

- 5 lb. of pork, beef or veal brisket diced in small pieces
- 5 ground garlic cloves
- ½ cup vinegar
- 1 tbsp ground oregano
- 1 tbsp ground peppermint
- 2 tbsp ground annatto (also called achiote) – optional
- 2 tbsp canola oil
- ½ tbsp sugar
- Dash of salt
- Dash of pepper (if desired)

PREPARATION:

1. Mix all the ingredients, except the oil, and place in the refrigerator, preferably the day before.

2. In a large frying pan, heat the oil, then sauté the meat slowly until done.

Chicken and Rice

- 3 chicken breasts
- 4 cups rice
- 1 large finely-chopped red onion
- 1 red pepper
- 6 garlic cloves
- 2 chopped green celery stalks
- 1 cup chopped carrots
- 2 chopped green onion stalks
- 1tbsp sugar
- 3 tsp canola or olive oil
- Dash of salt
- Dash of pepper

PREPARATION:

1. Cook chicken breast with two cups water and half of all the vegetables, except the green onions. Over medium heat, cook the ingredients until chicken is tender, add salt and pepper and 1 tbsp sugar. Let cool and shred chicken.

2. Cook rice as usual, using the water in which the chicken was boiled.

3. In large frying pan, add oil and uncooked vegetables and sauté for a few minutes.

4. Add chicken and rice slowly, then salt and pepper. Cook until all vegetables are tender and rice is cooked.

5. Serve with diced green onions on top.

Pork Ribs

INGREDIENTS

- 2 ½ lb pork ribs
- 6 medium potatoes cut in 4 pieces
- 4 mirliton cut in sticks
- Minced garlic
- 1 ½ cup water
- Salt
- 1 tbsp sugar

PREPARATION:

1. Rub the ribs with garlic and quickly fry in large saucepan, add the water, let it boil and then simmer for 25 minutes.

2. Add the vegetables. (Vegetables can be substituted for white beans or chick peas). Let simmer until vegetables are done.

Stuffed Loin

INGREDIENTS

- 4 lb beef or pork loin
- 4 boiled eggs
- ½ lb peeled potatoes
- 1 diced red bell pepper
- 2 small carrots cut in strips
- 1 tbsp Worcestershire sauce
- 1 tbsp sugar
- 1 tbsp achiote or annatto powder

PREPARATION:

1. Open beef or pork loin and stuff with the red bell pepper, slices of hard-boiled egg, carrot sticks and diced potatoes.

2. Wrap and tie with a cord, rub it with achiote or annatto powder, place in an oil-sprayed saucepan and cook over low or medium heat until done.

Flavored Guanacastecan Gallo Pinto

INGREDIENTS

- 2 cups of cooked beans (black or red beans) that have been fried with onions, pepper and cilantro
- 4 cups of cooked rice

PREPARATION:

1. Mix together rice and beans, place in a sauce pan and cook for about ten minutes.

2. Add black coffee, classic coke or sugar to enhance flavor (optional).

Vegetable Hash

INGREDIENTS

- 2 cups diced carrots
- 2 cups peeled diced potatoes
- 2 cups green beans cut into 1-inch pieces
- 2 cups diced mirliton
- 2 diced red peppers
- ½ cup diced cilantro
- ½ cup diced green onions
- ¼ cup diced red onions
- 2 ground garlic cloves
- 1 cup chicken broth
- 1 tbsp. sugar
- Dash of salt

PREPARATION:

1. Mix all the ingredients and simmer over low heat until ingredients are soft.

2. Serve hot and garnish with parsley.

Potato Hash

INGREDIENTS

- 2 ½ lb medium potatoes
- ½ cup diced onion
- 1 diced red bell pepper
- 3 peeled garlic cloves
- 1 cup beef broth
- 3 strained medium ripe tomatoes
- ½ lb hamburger beef
- 2 tbsp vegetable oil
- 1 tbsp achiote or annatto powder
- 1 cup cold water
- Salt and pepper

PREPARATION:

1. Peel potatoes and cut in small pieces, place them in a bowl with water so they don't become black.

2. In a saucepan, place the oil and achiote or annatto powder. Once it is dissolved add the onion, red pepper and garlic.

3. Fry for two minutes over medium heat, add the hamburger beef and cook for approx 5 minutes, making sure it does not stick to the bottom.

4. When the beef is cooked, mix potatoes with beef. Add tomatoes, beef broth and cook over low heat for about 15 minutes or until the potatoes are done.

Potato and Sausage Hash*

INGREDIENTS

- 2 ½ lb potatoes
- 1 ¼ lb sausage,
  beef or chicken
- 1 large onion
- 1 red pepper
- 1 cup fresh chopped cilantro

* In this recipe the sausage can be substituted with ground beef or chicken.

PREPARATION:

1. Boil potatoes with skin
   in salted water for about 15
   or 20 minutes.
   Drain the water,
   let the potatoes cool,
   peel and cut in small cubes.

2. In a large frying pan,
   place the sausage, onion,
   red pepper, and allow
   the onion to crystalize.
   Once the meat is cooked
   and the onion is transparent,
   add the potatoes and mix well.
   If desired, add salt, pepper
   and ½ tsp sugar.
   Cook until all ingredients
   are well blended then
   add the fresh cilantro.

Mirliton Stew

- 1 lb peeled, seeded and diced mirliton
- 3 tbsp olive oil
- 2 medium, thinly sliced garlic cloves
- 1 diced onion
- 1 large tomato chopped
- 1 red pepper diced
- ½ cup water
- Salt
- ½ cup heavy cream
- ½ Tb grated white cheese

PREPARATION:

1. Over medium heat, warm up oil, add the garlic and onion and fry until the onion is transparent. Add the mirliton, tomato, red pepper, add ½ cup water and 1 tbsp salt.

2. Cover, reduce heat to low and simmer, stirring occasionally until mirliton is soft and liquid has evaporated.

3. Serve hot with cream and grated cheese on top.

Easy Mashed Beans

- 1 can black bean soup (do not add water)
- 2 tbsp butter or olive oil
- 2 tbsp finely chopped onion
- ½ cup black coffee
- Dash of salt
- 1 tbsp sugar
- 2 tsp Worchestershire Sauce

PREPARATION:

1. Dissolve butter over low heat, add onion and crystalize, mix the undiluted bean soup stirring constantly and add the coffee, salt, sugar and Worcestershire sauce.

2. Let simmer until it is no longer liquidly. These mashed beans can be used as a side dish, a dip or as a spread on tortillas or bread.

Sweet Plantains with Cheese

INGREDIENTS

- 3 very ripe yellow plantains
- ½ lb mozzarella cheese

PREPARATION:

1. Peel plantains and cut in the middle, then cut lengthwise in ¼ inch slices.

2. Spread slices on lightly greased baking pan and top each plantain slice with sliced or shredded mozzarella cheese. Bake until plantains are cooked and cheese is melted.

Squash Delights

INGREDIENTS

- 2 lb squash. (Wash the peel, cut in approximately 1½ by 1½ inch pieces, remove the seeds and do not peel)
- 1 lb brown sugar
- 2 tsp cinnamon
- 6 cloves
- Dash of salt

PREPARATION:

1. Place the sugar in a large saucepan, add 2 cups water, cinnamon, cloves and the squash pieces, bring to a boil, lower temperature and simmer at very low heat until the squash in tender. Serve warm or cold.

Participants' Quotes

Name	Characteristic	Specific Traits
Dimas Sequeira Sequeira	Culture	Entrepreneurship
		Hard-working
	Personality	Collectivistic society
		Competence
		Hard-working
Estanislao Suárez Suárez	Culture	Fatalistic/Religion
	Personality and Culture	Belief that Future will be good
		Party dancing
		Respect for elders
	Personality	Collectivistic society
		Competence
		Competence
		Entrepreneurship

At 6 years of age, I was selling what older women would sell.

I loved baking to sell the products.

I enjoy when relatives and friends come to visit me.

I have seldom had to take even an aspirin.

I used to ride a horse for 12 hours to take things to be sold.

I do not govern anything I do and do not own anything;
God and my children are in charge of me
and God is the one that governs everything.

There is no need to move from place to place;
I have everything I need in this town.

I am a happy man and like to play guitars and dance.

I only married at 27 years of age
because my mother did not want me to get married.

I shared cows and vegetables and fruit with neighbors.

I managed and supervised my business and personal finances
up to 90 years of age.

I have never had a headache in my life.

I have always been an entrepreneur.

Name	Characteristic	Specific Traits
Francisca Rodríguez Sequeira	Culture	External attribution
		Fatalistic/Religion
		Fatalistic/Religion
		Positive emotion
		Respect for elders
	Personality	Deep religion
		Happiness
		Positive emotion
Jorge Vindas López	Culture	Respect for elders
	Personality and Culture	Lifestyle
		Pura Vida

God gives me everything I need or ask
for and it's very rare that he does not please me.

Life is like this. It was not meant to be that I would marry that man.

I had a husband that God had chosen for me.

My life was very peaceful, as my dad had a small farm
so there was never any need. He was never rude or harsh
with us and the whole family got along fine together
as did most people at that time.

It had gotten into my father's head that he wanted
to move the whole family to be closer to two daughters.

My life goes hand in hand with God and I have great internal peace.

I do not live out of sadness; I live out of happiness.
My children are excellent and God is also excellent with me.

I cannot complain about anything. I played at school
and then with friends, and mother was a very good, loving woman.

Centenarians were very obedient to their parents' requests.
Their children respect their parents' wishes no matter
how old the parents are now.

Centenarians have a simple lifestyle, live with the basics,
and have a piece of land, a roof over their head and food to eat.

Talking to a centenarian is as fascinating as reading a great book
you can't stop reading.

Name	Characteristic	Specific Traits
Jorge Vindas López	Personality	Happiness
		Openness
		Present orientation
		Self-discipline
José Bonifacio Villegas Fonseca	Culture	Religion
	Personality and Culture	Respect for elders
	Personality	Generosity
		Happiness
		Identity
		Positive emotion

Centenarians live in peace and are happy people.

Centenarians are good people who share with others.
They have been very generous throughout their lives.

Centenarians have a relaxed lifestyle and enjoy life.
They are happy and live in the now, stress-free.

Centenarians respect themselves in every aspect.
They take time to take a siesta after lunch
and nap during the day if they are tired.

Centenarians do not buy things they cannot afford.
They try to avoid complexities and stress in life.

Everything in this world gets solved by God.

I could not leave father until his death when I was 28 years old.

I have given all my possessions to my children,
so I do not have to worry about those things.

I have always liked to dance and be happy.

Happiness for me is to be with friends.

I am very proud of Nicoya and have never moved
from the place I was born.

I thank God for always being very friendly and I have lots of friends.

Name	Characteristic	Specific Traits
José Carlos Moraga	Culture	Avoiding conflict
		Collectivistic society
		Identity
		Respect for elders
	Personality	Generosity
Pablo Castillo Carrillo	Culture	Collectivistic society
	Personality	Happiness
		Identity
		Positive emotion
		Self-efficacy

Always buy with cash, and if someone gives you a hand, do not ask for his elbow.

Grandpa taught all of us about work values, not only the immediate family but also the godchildren and other relatives.

Always present was the concept of the family as a unity of collaboration, and values were taught through the group.

My identity was shaped by the way I was brought up and the people I grew up with.

Grandpa talked about respect for oneself, respect for others, solidarity and group unity.

In the afternoons, while getting my university course work done, I would go to my grandpa's house to spend time with him to learn from him.

Grandpa would help anyone that was needed money.

I get up at 5 a.m. and start walking and visiting friends that live nearby.

I live alone and in peace so that no one bothers me and I do not bother anyone.

I would like to be buried with mariachis.

I have never abandoned my place, Matina.

There is nothing more beautiful in life than friendship.

I learned to take care of myself, since I was very young.

Name	Characteristic	Specific Traits
Romualdo Álvarez Álvarez	Culture	Collectivistic society
		Religion
	Personality and Culture	Happiness
		Hard-working
Saúl Guzmán Salas	Personality	Happiness
	Culture	Dependable for others
		Identity
	Personality and Culture	Agreeable
		Deep religion
	Personality	Deep religion
		Hard-working
		Entrepreneurship

Our parents and we children worked together
to produce corn and beans.

I built my home right across from where I live now
and have always lived here.

God governs everything and no one and nothing has power over Him.

I have loved friends since childhood and love to party,
especially if there are guitars, marimbas and dancing.

I worked since I finished attending school after 3rd grade until I retired.

All my life, I have liked friends, liked to dance,
listen to music, and enjoyed a peaceful life.

I have for many years lived surrounded by my adult children;
three adult children still live with me.

Nicoya is a happy place to live. People like to dance
and marimba music makes for a great atmosphere.

I have been very friendly with everyone all my life
and I do not have enemies; I only have friends.

The only real friend is God and He is the only friend I can trust.

I pray from the bottom of my heart and ask God to help me.

I retired from business and farming when I was 80 years old.

I grew up in the business world.

Name	Characteristic	Specific Traits
 Trinidad Espinoza Medina	Personality and Culture	Deep religion
		Identity
	Personality	Collectivistic society
		Happiness

Square in front Nicoya Colonial Church

Quote

I pray every night asking God not to take me yet,
as I do not want to leave my children alone.

I love Nicoya and I was born here, so I will die in this region.

I love to have friends, women as well as men,
and these friends come and visit me; my friends make me happy.

I love to dance and my spirits get high when I listen to happy music.

Foto: © Cristina E. Díaz

Foto: © Alfredo Huerta Reyes

Elizabeth Lopez is a Costa Rican national with an Ed.D. in Counseling from George Washington University. At the World Bank, she was responsible for establishing and running an innovative mentoring program directly involving 6,000 officials which led to international speaking engagements, including keynote speaker at a European mentoring conference in Cambridge, at the World Health Organization in Geneva and Goldman Sachs. She has 40 years of experience in the field of well-being human development as a counselor, psychologist, consultant and lecturer. She has worked in this area in the United States, Indonesia, Switzerland, India and Central American countries, including Costa Rica where she was the psychologist on the 2007 Blue Zones™ expedition researching the reasons why Costa Ricans in the Nicoya Peninsula were among the longest living people in the world. She has augmented her educational training at Harvard and taught at several universities, including John Hopkins, George Washington and the University of Costa Rica. Elizabeth's interest in the blue zone of Costa Rica and its inhabitants is based on her lifelong relationship with this geographical area as her mother was from that part of the country. In recent years, she has continued her research on Costa Rica's centenarians with a focus on the interaction between culture, personality and longevity and presented on that topic at the 2017 World Forum on Blue Zones. Elizabeth now divides her time between living in Costa Rica and the United States with her American husband. She has four daughters and ten grandchildren.

info@happycentenarians.com

Curious if you'll make it to 100?

Take the quiz at **www.happycentenarians.com!**

A portion of the profit from this book will be donated to a
fund to support Costa Rica's centenarians.